Has Anybody Seen My Shoes?

By Danny Frasier

A story of faith, hope, and encouragement... and a little laughter thrown in for fun!

Has Anybody Seen My Shoes

© 2003 Danny Frasier

Edited by Mike G. Williams and Elma Peckinpaugh
Text preparation by Theda Llewellyn
Cover Art by Theda Llewellyn
Packaged by Pine Hill Graphics, Eugene, Or
Printed in the United States of America

Contents

Mike G. Williams writes about the author

Dear Reader,

Danny Frasier is the world's shortest comedian and motivational speaker. At two-foot eleven inches tall, his body may not stand out above the crowd but his tremendous attitude does. Danny can make you laugh. Danny can make you cry. But for the most part, he will make you realize that you can achieve your goals if you work hard and consistently. He speaks with an upper New York accent and sings with a voice reminiscent of the late Hank Williams. Whether it's sharing his funny stories, singing his songs, or pretending to lie under the wheels of a bus filled with senior citizens, Danny will steal your heart. He does that real well. He's the kind of guy who has never met a stranger. His great attitude has allowed him to walk where others in his condition have not. He has shared the stage with everyone from world famous recording artists to governmental dignitaries. You will be motivated, challenged, and encouraged by the wit, charm, and positive attitude of this amazing young man.

It has been my privilege to get to know this bright young man over the past few years. After reading this book I know that you will feel that same privilege. While working with Danny on this manuscript I have come to really love and respect this guy. I know the world will be seeing and hearing a lot more from him in the future years.

Mike G. Williams
Editor

Learn more about Danny Frasier at www.dannyfrasier.com
Learn More about Mike G. Williams at www.christiancomedian.com

I don't know Danny very well. But, it doesn't take long to see he's got a big heart. I met him at a comedian's convention. I'll never forget the night he took the stage. He didn't walk up there like the rest of the comedians. But, when he opened his mouth and started talking...he stood as tall. Danny is funny. Danny is positive. Danny has a great message. He has traveled through trials we'll, probably, never have to walk through. He's learned a lot along the way. And he'll tell anybody who has the time to listen.

And, did I mention...the boy is FUNNY!

Seeing that this is a book forward, let me mention the book. The copy I have is still on my computer, so what you are seeing must look better than what I have. But nevertheless, I can see a good work in progress here. The chapters are filled with funny stories and serious motivation. Throughout this book you may laugh, you may cry, or you may simply giggle as you sip your hot chocolate. But, be careful, you might choke! So, put down the hot chocolate before you start.

I hope that you will be motivated! Motivated to thankfulness. Moved to compassion. Encouraged to stop limiting your own thinking and accelerate your own personal growth.

Danny, keep telling folks the good news. God loves us all. Those who are broken on the outside and all of us who are broken on the inside. God loves broken people. Even those who don't know they're broken, He loves. We all need to hear your message. It truly is GOOD NEWS!

Mark Lowry

Introduction

Hi! My name is Danny and these are my stories, but you own the book. You bought it so you can do what you want with it, but I want to offer a little advice on how to read it. Put it on your nightstand and peruse a chapter or two when you need a little lift in your spirit. This is not a book about handicaps, or troubles, or tragedies. This is a book about finding strength in the midst of tough situations. My tough situations and your tough situations. I hope that you will do just that.

I sure hope you like to laugh. I do! I laugh every day. It's good for you. Sometimes I laugh to keep from crying and sometimes I laugh because the world is a funny place to live. I believe that God has placed humor all around us. It is a vitamin! It is an antibiotic for "Mondays". And seeing that we get at least fifty-two Mondays each year, I believe we need to take the laughter pill every day; and believe me, I know something about pills. I have swallowed enough pills in my day to choke a man twice my size which is probably closer your size. So in a way, we are not really so different.

In fact, I think that you will find that we are very similar in many ways. Maybe you don't have what most of the world would call a physical handicap, but I'll bet that you have struggled with many of the emotions that I have. I'll bet that you have been hurt. I'll bet that you have been disappointed. I'll bet that you wonder about your future. It is my desire that the stories from my life will be an encouragement to you. I hope they will make you laugh, and maybe even cry, but only at the appropriate times. These stories are about my life. And it aint over! So I expect you to buy volume two in a couple of years.

Finally, I want to say thanks for buying this book. I need the money! I'm saving up to buy a Volkswagen Bug. One of the convertible models! The car is just "me" okay? So go to my website and order more books and CD's for your friends so I can afford to get the automatic transmission model. Trust me, you don't want me to have to do a handstand to shift the gears while your kids are in the lane next to me.

By the way, if you ever see me at the mall, don't be afraid to say "hello". Plop down on the floor and we will talk for a while. Seriously, don't just stand there, plop down on the floor, I'm tired of getting kinks in my neck from conversing vertically. You really don't want to be responsible for my having a chiropractic condition. I could get mad and hit you in the kneecaps! So consider the health of your kneecaps and don't make me mad!

Danny Frasier

July 23,1984

It's against all odds, but it's a chance we've got to take.
-Phil Collins

The year was 1984 and Pride in the name of Love by U2, Against All Odds (Take a look at me now) by Phil Collins, Victims by Culture Club, and I want to be a Freak by Queen were blaring across the airwaves. Yes, other than the first two it was a pretty poor year for music, but the hits of the year were definitely defining, or at least titling the generation.

Today the nation is reeling from the news of a horrible shooting at a McDonalds restaurant in San Ysidro, California, five days ago, as James Oliver Huberty walked into a restaurant and opened fire, killing twenty-one people. The only break from that media frenzy has been a breaking story this morning of the dethroning of the current Miss America for a moral failure. Like so many other days, I'm sure there were a lot of other stories of special interest that didn't even make the news. But for most people life went on in the rest of the world, almost untouched by the news of the hour.

Another story that didn't make the news was mine. Well if it did, they have never told me about it. Nobody saved any newspaper clippings for me. I guess I should ask someone about that. If it had made the headlines, they would have read "Rochester New York... little boy was born fighting for his life." At one pound, two ounces the doctors didn't have a lot of hope for me. Today, for someone in my condition they might feel differently. Medical care has come a long way in two decades, but that was 1984. With all the classic signs of Fetal Alcohol Syndrome; born prematurely, small head, no bridge to my nose, wide-set eyes, and bone deformities (my legs were wrapped up in knots underneath me), I was asthmatic, allergic to almost every known anti-biotic, deaf in my left ear, little hearing in my right, and I had a plethora of other conditions.

Doctors like to deliver healthy babies. The whole birth process is supposed to be about celebration, but this was one of those situations that made doctors wince, and nurses shed a tear. This was one of those situations that made the theologians ask why. But there were few questions this day. My birth mother was addicted to drugs and alcohol. For children in my position this is quite common.

None of us has choice as to where or to whom we are born. If we did, most of us certainly would have picked another way. It does not matter whether you are from a rich home or a poor home, educated family or illiterate one, we would all probably like to change a few things about our early childhood. I am no different. But we don't have a choice, so I spent the next three months tied to ventilators and respirators and a dozen other contraptions that to this day I could not pronounce correctly. I imagine I looked as if I had been assimilated into the Borg. But I imagine only the Star Trek fans would understand what that meant!

Greatness is not in where we stand, but in what
direction we are moving. We must sail sometimes with the
wind and sometimes against it - but sail we must,
and not drift, nor lie at anchor.
-*Oliver Wendell Holmes*

Winter Is Coming

Four out of five of the dentists are doing 80% of the Dental work in this country and I don't think that is fair. -Tim Jones

The State of New York was obviously not going to let me go home with my birth mother, at least not immediately, so they began the tedious process of finding a foster home for me. It is one thing to try to find a foster home for a kid with all the goodies, but quite another to find a home for a child attached to life support. The lady in charge of finding me a home was Mary Farren. After many years of finding homes for kids in tragic circumstances she went to the phone for me. She called the twelve year veterans to the foster care system, Sandi and Rod Frasier. Sandy and Rod had seen it all. They've had at least fifty children pass through their doors in the years before me. They have experienced all of the heartbreak of raising a kid for a year and then seeing the courts send them back into horrible situations, because a judge wanted to give a drug addicted parent another chance to get it right. They have watched the heartbreak of seeing the same children tossed around from home to home for most of their formative years. Rod and Sandi are not hardened, nor are they soft, rather they are realists. They understand the unique situations that most foster children are in and they try to help.

Mary called the Frasier house and explained the situation to Sandi. There was a uneasy crackle in Mary's voice; and I'm told that you could tell this was not one of those calls that she was told she was going to have to make when she took the job twenty years ago. "We have this little boy," her voice growing ever more shaken, "I can't ask you to take him... They don't expect him to survive." Foster parents are used to getting strange requests in the middle of the night. Calls involving problematic children who need to be placed in yet another foster home. But this was different, they were being asked to take home a child to die. How can anyone expect a person to do that? How can any agency really ask a person to take home a helpless little child to care for until they expire? But somebody has to do it. Every day around this country somebody is asked to do it. Whether that be for F.A.S. children or AIDS babies, it has to happen.

Sandi said that she would go by the hospital and at take

a look at me. She did. Now I don't remember those first visits, but I am told that when she saw my big round eyes, she new she couldn't leave me there. Boy, I'm sure glad I was born with eyes! I certainly couldn't impress her with my cute little legs. The doctors informed Sandi of my prognosis - it was not good. I was not expected to survive the winter. If I did survive, most assuredly I would be deaf, retarded, and in a wheelchair the rest of my life. There were a number of other horrendous possibilities, but it would be a waiting game to see what was to develop next. But nevertheless, my big beautiful doe eyes, I think she called them beautiful, would not let Sandi leave me there! I had a home.

The Fraisers went through the process of learning how to care for me. They learned about the unique feeding procedures and everything else that goes along with a special needs child. And before I knew it I was in a car and on my way to my very first home. They kept me in a wicker laundry basket. They say it was because I was so small and needed constant care, which I'm sure was true, but it might have been because you would not want to invest that much into a child in my condition. I mean that monetarily and emotionally. But who could blame them? Who could blame anyone? According to what the doctors had said, I would not be with them for that long. Remember, it would be a miracle if I lasted the winter.

If the suspense is killing you right now, let me say, "The

doctors were wrong." I mean, hey, I am writing a book right now, think about it. I made it! Eighteen years later, I'm alive! But my journey was not over, and neither was theirs. I was a very sick baby and had to be fed every twenty minutes' round the clock. I would still like to eat that way, but nobody seems to want to comply to my desires anymore. I was allergic to every formula known to man and most antibiotics. I could not get near any fur bearing animals and a good many foods were on my black list. Hey, a picture of a fish tank could give me a rash! I'm glad that's over!

Our achievements are shaped by the terrain of our lives
and the strength of the foundations we set. In building
the life we've imagined, we must be true to our beliefs, dare
to be ethical, and strive to be honorable; for integrity is the
highest ground to which we can aspire.

-John Maxwell

Teachers and Therapy, It Never Changes

When you're riding in the Hindenburg... who really cares if you got a window seat? -Mike G. Williams

Before long I had passed that critical condition and the medical community began to think that I might actually make it. Surprise, surprise, surprise! I've always said that you can't keep a good man down! Teachers and therapists came to the house everyday. They worked with my arms and hands. They worked with my muscles and frame. They worked with my mind. How they did this I do not know, but they tell me they did. So if you do feel that there is any weirdness in this brain, it is their fault. I was corrupted by the evil therapist! I think her name was Cybil!

They started me in a program called the Infant Stimulation Intervention Program. Teachers would come to my house every day to work on my speech, physical therapy, and overall development. The Frasiers were told to expose me to light, sound, smells, anything to encourage me to thrive. Exposure to light can be stimulating! It sure beats darkness. They exposed me to sound and motion. They chose Raffi videos. And, of course, Peter, Paul, and Mary music. I must have worn out fifteen copies of Puff the Magic Dragon which to this day I still hear playing over and over in my sleep. Over and over like a broken record I hear old Puff! It's like riding It's A Small World at Disney World. You can get off the ride, but the song continues to play, over and over and over. But my therapist says it will go away eventually! No, it was a good song.

When I was in my chair the only thing that could keep my attention was to put me in front of the organ. I certainly don't remember this, but they say that I was picking out songs on the organ at twenty-two months. But really, if you're stuck in front of an organ all the time you're going to do something with it! And seeing that I didn't have a chainsaw, I pecked at the keys a little. I never really learned to play it well. I mean no offense to the organ players, but I just never really wanted to be remembered as the World's Smallest Organ Player. My Mom often jokingly says, "I believe that music was instrumental in Danny's survival... no pun intended!"

I don't remember anything about my exposures to

smell. And that's ironic because they say that your memory is closely connected to smells. I guess they didn't ask me to smell anything really memorable. But to this day, I have never appreciated the smells that often come from babies rooms. You know, that combination of baby powder, warm milk, and flying melba toast - Nasty!

My foster parents took me everywhere they went - well along with the six other children in the family. Yes, traveling with us was like an old episode of The Partridge Family, and yes, I played the part of Danny! There were times when people would whisper about us as we went by. I think they thought we were a cult or something, with all the kids; but we were not. Sandi was a Methodist and Rod was a Baptist, so they settled into a Lutheran Church. I guess they thought it was a good compromise. My parents aren't real big on denominations or denominationalism. And with that many kids, making it to church every week was not always possible - yet they always taught me right from wrong. And they taught me that it is our own personal relationship with God that matters most.

When I was at church I liked to sit up front near the organ speakers and listen to the music. I would sit in a big green Tupperware bowl and just spin to the music. Being mostly deaf, I could hear things better if I was close to the speaker. I could also feel the music vibrate through the floor.

I really liked music and still do. It was soothing to me. It made me smile. The low notes on the organ would shake my little Tupperware bowl and I would smile. Well they tell me that I did. I didn't actually receive the gift of a photographic memory until I was three years old, or maybe it was when I was five...I can't seem to remember.

Some people have to learn the hard way that it doesn't pay
to get discouraged. Positive thinking is a choice, and
by keeping our eyes focused on a bright future we will
not be distracted by the negativity around us.

-Danny Frasier

Adopted, I've Got A Family Now

I may have never gotten picked first for the baseball team. In fact I wouldn't be picked for most teams at all. But I was picked for the Frasier Team! Despite my handicaps, batting average, and suspected outcome, I was picked to be a part! That feels real good. -Danny Frasier

A lot of people want to hear all the details about my adoption. They want to know all the details about the event. Let's be honest, I was two years old. I don't remember a whole lot about being two! In fact from about zero to four are all just a blur! I have lots of pictures from those years and I have been told lots of stories, but for this book I will leave it at that.

My editor said he wanted more information on my adoption and biological family. He then wanted me to expound on how I felt about being adopted. I wrote back to him, "To tell you the truth I had to work on this one. I never really think too much about it. This is my forever family. They are all I've known and I am grateful to God for the day He sent my parents to me. I know that it was His plan for me to be with the Frasiers. We've had good times and bad times just like any family, but to know that my parents had a choice to take me home or walk away makes our bond very strong and special."

Adoption is a very special thing. If you are an adopted person you understand that. When you consider that you were chosen, it makes you feel very special. It does not matter whether you were chosen from a horrible background or a good one. It does not matter whether you know your biological parent(s) or not. It matters little if you were adopted by strangers or family. If you were adopted, you were specially chosen. You were hand selected. The judge made your adoptive parents declare some large promises over you, promises that biological children never had made over them. If you're adopted, be thankful. You may never fully know the tragedies that you were saved from, and that is probably a good thing - a very good thing.

The stepping stones of my life have been rough
and painful at times...and although I would not want to
walk them again...they have brought me to this very place...
and for that I am extremely grateful.

-Mike G. Williams

The Next Few Years

You have to accept the fact that some days you're a pigeon and
some days you're a statue.
Welcome to the real world. -Ken Davis

Time passes more quickly than we want to admit. It seems like only yesterday I was in those critical years. Fortunately I don't remember a lot about them. Maybe that is good. You understand, right? But I do remember some things, a And I seem to remember the fun things most of all.

It wasn't long after my second birthday when the doctors concluded they would never be able to straighten my legs, and opted to take them off.. Now they never really asked me how I felt about this. At two years old they kind of leave you out of the whole process. They left me some short little stumps in hopes that they would be able to attach some kind of artificial prosthesis at some point in the future. But as you, know if you have seen me, that idea never really worked out. It's not that we didn't try. We did...many times. But Sometimes things are just not meant to be and I have come to terms with that. And it's hard to be the World's Shortest Motivational Speaker when you are six foot tall! It just wouldn't look right! It would be a bit anti-climactic. I would have to change my moniker to Formerly: The World's Shortest Motivational Speaker.

At two and three years old, my favorite activity was going to the store with my mom. I was so small that I would often climb out of a grocery cart and onto the counter. They tell me the cashier would reach for the milk and grab me instead. I always wonder what the scanner would read if I ever got scanned. Probably ham! Yes, I had a lot of fun back in those early days. Have you ever seen the warnings on grocery carts? The warnings regarding the proper way to place a child in the grocery cart? They tell you where the feet are supposed to go, and where they are not supposed to go. They tell you not to place a child inside the cart because it could tip over. Well all the warnings left me in a lurch. I couldn't be inside the cart because that was dangerous, and I couldn't be in the seat because I had no legs to strap down. What's a mom to do? So we reached a compromise. I rode horizontally on my stomach under the basket of the grocery cart. There was no warning placard about this and it allowed me to have a little fun, too. In fact, this allowed me to have a lot of fun.

Lying under the cart I would use my hands to move the cart around when my mom didn't have her hands on the cart handle. She would turn to pick up a grocery item, and I would roll the cart down the aisle. Sometimes I would bump into other carts and pull my hands in really fast. If the bottom of the cart was full of groceries the people I hit did not see me. They thought that my mom just pushed her cart into them. Then when she looked toward the cart and hollered, "Danny quit doing that! I've told you a hundred times not to do that," the people would think that she was delusional; which living with me could probably make you that way. I had a lot of fun in those early days in the grocery store.

You can learn a lot lying under a grocery cart. You can see how well they really clean the floors, you can tell if peoples socks match without them knowing it, sometimes you can even see people's underwear from that perspective. I know I shouldn't say that, but it is true. I wanted to sing "I See London - I see France," every time we went shopping. But my mom wouldn't let me.

In the movie entitled Dead Poet Society, Robin Williams plays a rogue teacher in an elite boys school. At one point in the movie he asks each boy to stand on top of the desk and view the class from a different perspective. Some of them were really quite hesitant. Eventually each one of them participated in the activity. It was simple lesson that taught them the great need to view things from a different point of view. That is a great lesson we all need to learn.

It is so easy to be critical of another person's position in life. But we become much more grace filled in our assessments of others when we see things from their perspective. The old saying goes, "Don't criticize someone until you walk a mile in there shoes." Admittedly, I could not walk in your shoes; but then again I don't think you could walk on your hands in my gloves very easily either. Well maybe if you were a gymnast or a break-dancer, but it is so rare to find a break-dancing gymnast anymore that I think I am safe in making that assumption!

So the next time you wonder why they have to have all those handicapped spots up by the door, consider how you would feel if you were unable to walk. The next time you see someone on the side of the road with a cardboard sign, consider what it would be like if you were homeless. The next time you hear someone speaking in broken English, consider how you would feel trying to communicate in a foreign language. And the next time you see someone in a wheelchair blocking so much of your aisle, consider shopping for your groceries from a chair yourself. And by all means, crawl under a grocery cart for a few weeks. You may just get a better understanding of someone else's world and you may just get a glimpse of some funny underpants in the process!

By the way, I am personally trying to figure why you people with feet walk so slow! You've got the potential for huge strides...move it! Life's too short to spend it loafing around in the hall. I want to add that we haven't completely given up on me walking tall someday either. With the technological advances being made each day, I may one day have some type of walking assistance. But they better not be made by Tupperware! I wouldn't mind being the first real bionic man!

Unless you try to achieve something beyond what you have
already mastered, you will never grow.
It takes little or no effort to remain stagnant!
-Gordon Douglas

Hold On Tight

My Dad used to put my Slip-n-Slide on the gravel driveway. He believed it would teach me that life was fun but sometimes painful. -Mike G. Williams

I played with all the toys that you probably did, in my formative years. Well, maybe not a bike. But I did turn it upside down and pretend. And nobody turns a crank any faster than me! But if you think getting a shoe lace caught in a chain is bad, try getting your shirt sleeve caught in one! It aint pretty! I loved to build with Legos, and truth be told, I still enjoy an occasional plastic building project!

My dad Rod used to put me into one of those spring mounted jumpers! The kind that you hang from a door jamb and let the kid kick his feet and bounce up and down. I hated that. I could not kick my feet and make it bounce. So, I would try and climb the cables and springs. Eventually he took the chair off the spring and I would simply hold onto the metal bar and do pull ups. There I was at two and three years old hanging by my white knuckles five feet in the air. I looked like a brown-eyed monkey! I don't know if monkeys have brown eyes though. Maybe I should check it out before I say that. But those pull ups helped me develop muscularly during those early years.

My friend Jeremy and I were inseparable as kids. Growing up in that suburban town of Hilton, New York, we had lots of fun playing in the snow. My foster mom, Sandi, would put me in a large plastic bag to keep me dry, and off I would go into the snow. If the wind caught me right, the bag would fill with air and I would wind up half way across my neighbors yard. But those bags did make for an economical snow suit.

We received a fair amount of snow in that area of the country and we kids loved it. Mom would give me a spatula and I would dig big holes in the snow. I was pretty good at it! Nobody rocks a spatula better than me. I would dive into a snow bank, head and spatula first. Once I actually dug a deep hole and fell in head first. I couldn't get out! Fortunately they found me in time. After surviving everything else at that age, the last thing I wanted them to say at my eulogy was, "Buried alive in two feet of snow." I think those days in the snow have thoroughly prepared me in the event I am ever caught in an avalanche. I know there is not a huge chance that it will happen where I live in Alabama, but it could. In my four short years in Alabama I have learned that just about anything can happen in this state.

All of our lives are preparation for something. We play sports, experience a tough situation, survive a malady, or sit through five hours of Karaoke, and it is all preparation for something. I often wonder what my life has been preparing me for. Have my childhood experiences been preparing me for a divinely predestined position? I hope so. It sure better have been for a purpose! If not, I am going to be really mad. Watch those kneecaps again! And your life too has been a preparation. You may not know what it is yet: Doctor, Lawyer, Indian Chief, Comedian, Motivational Speaker, Fireman, Grief Counselor, Loving Husband, Good Wife, and the list could go on. I believe that your life, the good times and bad, the games and the jobs, have been preparing you for a unique purpose. I know that some of those times of preparation have included horrible schools to attend. I know that some of those educational processes have taken much longer than you really wanted them to take. And unfortunately, I know that you are not through them all yet. Sorry. But wait - wait and keep learning. And one day, if you pay attention, you will know why. Pay attention because you don't want to miss the opportunity to fulfill your destiny. That would be a shame. But I think you will be given another chance. I believe that time is always trying to give us another chance to find our place in this world. The important thing is that we don't miss it.

The quality of my life is not determined by what happens to me, rather by how I react to what happens; not by what life brings me, but by the attitude I confront it with.

-*Danny Frasier*

I'm Not Handicapped

I know there are people in this world who do not love their fellow man, and I hate people like that! -Tom Lehrer

The first time I participated in any type of Special Olympics I was five years old. Now most people want to combine all Special Olympic events into one category. There are actually a few different kinds of Special Olympics. There are games for those who are stricken with some type of mental handicap and there are games for those who have a physical handicap. I participated in the New York State Games for the Physically Challenged. It was a thrill for me to participate and I learned a lot. Every time you participate in an event like that you come away moved and challenged.

At five years old, I was enamored with it all. I couldn't get over all the kids who were just like me. I was amazed at all the people coming in the doors with crutches and wheelchairs. There were people with no arms or legs and every conceivable variation along that theme. I remember asking my dad, "Are they all handicapped?" He explained that they were. "Dad, am I handicapped? Am I?" With great wisdom, in what was a defining moment of my life, Dad responded, "No, you're not handicapped, you're special!" Wow, I'm glad he said that, because I would sure hate to be handicapped. So from that moment on I never thought of myself as handicapped. I was special! Maybe we need to start looking at our little quirks as unique nesses rather than handicaps. Maybe if we considered ourselves as special we would quit looking at our can't and start looking at our can. Maybe if we considered ourselves special we would see possibilities where impossibilities once were.

My good friend often says, "Mom told me I was special... Just like everybody else!" The truth is that we are all special. We are all different. We have all come from varied backgrounds of tough set-backs, improbabilities, and steep mountains climbed or fallen down. I think we should quit comparing ourselves to each other and start appreciating the singularity of our own experiences. We are special...and so is everyone else!

Did I mention that I was an NYSGPC Gold medallist? Yeah, many times over. Archery was one. I had to sit on my dad's back to keep the bow from hitting the ground, but I hit the target! I was a regular Robin Hood. Though I wouldn't be caught dead in tights! Shot-put was my specialty. The development of my very muscular upper torso (pardon the slight moment of pride) allowed me to do very well in that category. I also did great in bowling. Which I believe is a requirement for "fitting in" here in Oneonta, Alabama! You have to hunt, bowl, and drive a truck! Hey, two out of three aint bad! I was also a very strong swimmer and I have a very shallow draft. Draft is a nautical term that basically means I didn't have a lot of torso in the water resisting the water and motion. And if you think I look wild doing these things you are probably right. But it doesn't compare to watching me pole vault! Yep! I have done that also. Somebody once commented that watching me pole vault was like watching an ant play a game of Pixy-Stix. I would beg to differ with them.

When I say that I'm not handicapped, I'm right and I am wrong. In comparison to others, I may need to find another way to do something, but in comparison to me, you may have to find another way to do something. Compared to the birds, we are all handicapped. Can you fly? No? Awe, want a special white license plate that has a blue half circle in your buttocks region? Handicapped plates and signs always make me laugh. The picture doesn't represent a wheelchair, it looks more like a fat guy sitting on a cat. Can you dive under the ocean and swim with the fish for an extended length of time without artificial respiration devices? I didn't think so. I had a feeling that no Hokkido Pearl divers would be reading this book! So compared to fish we all handicapped!

Handicaps happen when we compare and measure ourselves according to another persons standard. I mean no disrespect to those who feel differently than me. The nature of what I am saying allows for us all to have differing views, as well as talents. It is just that I refuse to be measured against anyone but me! Remember, I'm special! And so are you. I got in trouble once at school when a teacher almost insisted that I wear a set of artificial legs that had been donated for me. I think the first owner must have been about six foot tall! You could hang drywall with these stilts! "C'mon, I'm getting a nosebleed up here!" Some of these prosthesis can be quite cumbersome and uncomfortable, and some can be downright inoperable! I told the teacher, "I'll wear my plastic legs if you'll walk on your hands... I mean no disrespect sir...just putting things into perspective!" I guess I was a little hard on him.

It would be a defining moment in your life if you started living up to your own potential and quit trying to live up to mine. What are you to become? How far can you go? What mountain do you want to climb? What giant do you want to slay? How deep do you want to dive? How high do you want to fly? You say that you can't fly, aye? How do you know?

Have you ever flapped your arms and leaped off the couch? For a moment you are flying! Well at least you're flying for a moment, before you experience a crash landing. The movie Toy Story has a great line that comes to mind right now. Buzz claims that he can fly. He leaps from the top of a dresser and begins to be tossed around by every possible item imaginable, including a few revolutions on the ceiling fan. It was an amazing display of lucky airmanship. The other toys applauded, while Woody, the antagonistic character commented, "That's not flying, that's falling with style." Aren't we all simply falling with style?

One mans flight is another mans folly, but who cares. They ran the Wright brothers out of North Carolina and now they dare to put "First in Flight" on their license tags. Hypocrites! Be yourself. Don't let anyone compare you to others, and quit comparing yourself to others. Push yourself to be all that you can be. Be diligent, be committed, because you are special - just like me! Now get out there and fall with style!

Losing is really only losing if you did not give
it your best effort! I will certainly not allow
mere apathy to be my greatest nemesis.

-Danny Frasier

Everyone Should Be In The Olympics

Even a clock that is not working is right twice a day.
-A Polish Proverb

We could use a few more games at the Olympics. How about hot dog eating? As if the Sumo Wrestlers don't do that before each match anyway. Just tape their dinner warm up and you have a match! Or what about finger painting? Or finger pointing for that matter? Many people are really good at that! Or chainsmoking? The French could win this one without having to bribe their own judges. The winner could receive a golden oxygen tank to hang around his neck instead of a medal. And let's combine the grace of figure skating with the violence of hockey. Tanya Harding could be the team captain. She would be a natural! And miniature golf! That's what we need to add. Maybe I could talk the Olympic Committee into it. Who knows? It could happen.

In a world where the corporate gold goes mainly to those who fight, claw, scratch, gouge, lie, cheat, and/or steal their way to the top, and the Olympic gold goes only to the best physical specimens, the Special Olympic type events demonstrate a fantastic alternative success model. Everybody should attend one at least once in their life. It would do them a world of good. Now, I've got cable and I watch ESPN. I've seen the major sporting events of our year. I have seen the great athletes battle it out during Olympic frenzies every few years. I applaud their efforts, and admire their ability to push themselves beyond the normal limit. And I can proudly say that in spite of the illegitimate votes of a few French judges, our "USA" boys and girls do it as well as anyone! But I do tend to like the Olympic alternatives. First of all, accolades are given for effort. And while you may not go home with a gold medal, you will go home rewarded for your effort. You will go home with the understanding that you were a winner any-time you gave it your all. And you don't see coaches scream-ing at their kids, trying to get a child to live out their own unfulfilled fantasy. You don't have a lot of parents trying to live their sports dreams vicariously through their child, and most favorably, you see athletes that care more about each other than they do crossing the finish line.

At these Olympic events it is not unusual to see a run-ner fall. It happens all the time. But it is also not unusual to see the entire pack of runners go back to help that person to their feet, and encourage them to go on. Wouldn't it be great if life could be like that? Not to encourage failure, but rather to encourage success. Because that is what it is... the encouragement of success. At these Olympic events, success is in the person - not the achievement! I guess I understand that in a competitive free market society there has to be competition, strong competition. Stockholders would not want to own a company that was all about making friends and giving stuff away. But apart from that scenario, wouldn't the world be a finer place to live if we were more concerned with people than we were with things? You can disagree with me if you want, but it's my book!

We all win, when one wins. Stephen Covey has often referred to this as a "win - win situation." I'm looking to connect my life with people who want to strap themselves to each other and climb the mountains that cannot be climbed on their own. Therein lies the greatest of all victories! This is the greatest success. The sum is greater than the parts. Together we can see our potential multiplied rather than simply added.

Change is life giving...it helps us grow into something
greater than we already are. Any metamorphosis is
painful...but it sure beats living in a cocoon.

-*Steven Smith*

Big Bad Turtles

There is a fine line between fishing and just standing in the water and looking wet and stupid and hungry. -Johnny Roberts

My dad and mom loved to go camping. I think they would have rather stayed in a hotel, but there were seven of us kids and they weren't rich people. So we went camping in Vermont. They were real good about spending individual time with each of us. So each day a different child would make the trip up the mountain to the secret lake. We looked forward to it every year. Especially me. At eight years old, I was considering becoming a pro bass fisherman. Hey, a boy can dream can't he? So up the mountain I went with all my tackle in tow. We arrived at the lake and had it all to ourselves. The day of fishing went well.

My first fish of the day was a five pound bass, and it was

the fightingest fish I had ever latched a hook into. This fish wanted to live! And live badly! The others I had caught came in relatively easy on my Zebco 202 fishing reel combo, but this one caught me off balance. Before I could release the drag and I found myself face down the old wooden peer, but I never let go of the pole! My dad grabbed me by the nap of my neck and righted me, I held on for the fight of my life. It may not seem like much to you, but when you're only forty pounds and have to balance on two small twigs, it's a battle. So with my Dad holding tightly to my collar I reeled in my prize. I never mounted the fish, but I did save the splinters from that old peer!

My dad was holding so tightly I could barely inhale, but the adrenaline flowing, I didn't need air. I landed that fish like Orlando Wilson! I put the fish on my stringer and tossed out another cast. Surely if there was a five pound fish in there, a ten pound fish would be next. But there was not. I waited and waited but there weren't any. Then I noticed that the stringer holding my trophy catch was being pulled for all it was worth. My dad grabbed for it and lifted it out of the water. The largest snapping turtle I had ever seen was dangling from the end, and trying to swallow my prize catch. I guess I wasn't the only one fishing that day.

We fished on. It must have been about ten minutes later when we heard an awful racket coming up the trail and two young hooligans' came frolicking into the pond. They splashed around and made all kinds of racket. Did they not know I was fishing? Did they not realize that I was there first? Did they not realize that I was about to land a ten pound bass? Did they not realize that they were dealing with possibly the next Bassmaster top contender? I doubt it! If they knew those things they would certainly get out of the pond. If they had any sense they would know the fish won't bite if these hooligans turned the pond into there own private Wet and Wild. So after about five "nibbleless" minutes I had had enough. So I hollered, "Do you know there are big snapping turtles in this pond?" "Yeah, we know," they shouted, undisturbed by my obvious warning. I stood up tall on my hands where they could see my stumpy legs dangling and said, "Well you better get out of there, look what they did to me last summer!" These guys would have given Peter a run for his money as they almost walked on water getting out of that pond! Up the mountain trail they ran like they had seen a ghost. You could hear them shouting the whole way. I would have loved to have been there when they tried to tell their parents what they saw. I imagine they got grounded for lying about the kid who lost his legs to a snapping turtle! It serves them right for ruining the fishing and my chances for a Vermont bass record!

Although I would not recommend being legless to

everyone, there are times when you can use it to have a little fun. The key to keeping a good attitude about our life situations is to have fun with your condition. I often open my speeches by walking up on the stage on my hands. The crowd can easily see that I have no legs. I get real serious and say, "Listen to me... Never play games with the lawnmower!" For a second they think about what I have said and then break into laughter. Sometimes I tell the crowd that I never took up smoking because my mom said it would stunt my growth. Hey, at thirty-five inches you can't afford to take any chances. I want to ride the roller coaster at Hershey Park someday!

Learn to laugh at your circumstances. If you can find a sliver of laughter during your hard times it will make those hard times easier. Certainly it does not make pain or hardship go away, but it does make the inevitable journey a lot more tolerable.

The Powerful current of a rushing river is not diminished
because it is forced to flow underground...
the purest water is that stream that burst into sunlight after
it has fought its way through solid rock.

-Gloria Gaither

A genuine positive attitude is like the course of a mighty
river...it may be diverted, but never stopped...
it may pool momentarily,
but it will eventually force its way to its destination.

-Danny Frasier

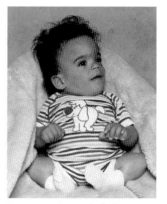

Danny at 10 month, before surgery — 1985

Danny getting his scooter board — 2 years old

Danny at age 3 — 1987

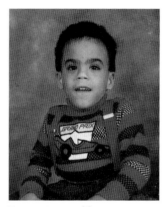

Danny 4 years old

Danny and family at adoption of 5 of his siblings — 1994

Danny Playing with Peter
Yarrow — 2001

Danny and friend at Junior
Prom — 2003

Danny on stage with Alabama — 2003

Danny and dad with gold medals
from New York State Games for
Physically Challenged

Danny and Mr. Frawley, teacher
and special friend

Danny in Cleveland Marching Band — 2004

Danny with guitar — 2004

Danny at book signing — 2006

Danny and Dad — 2006

Danny and his truck — 2010

Danny singing at Cleveland Baptist Church — 2006

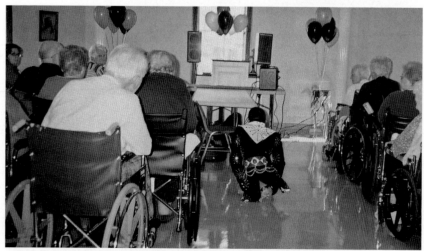

Danny doing Elvis at Hanceville Nursing Home — 2010

The Hokey Pokey

If you know what I mean, I don't need to explain. It goes without saying, if you know what I mean. So what more can I say?
-Steven Banks

In grade school we had to dance. It was part of the physical education curriculum. When I say dance, I don't mean hip, cool, contemporary dances - we are not talking about Soul Train here. I'm talking about square dancing, and doing the Hokey-Pokey. Do you remember that awful song? I hated that song. "Put your left hand in, pull your left hand out, do the Hokey-Pokey, and turn yourself about." I would balance myself on the desk and sing along with everyone else in the room. I was good with the hands part. I could do the neck part. I could even do the turn around, but the right foot-left foot gave me a bit of a problem. In today's equal access society, I imagine I could have had the ACLU require the school remove those lines from the song. Or maybe we could have declared the song to be unconstitutional! But if we eliminate everything that eliminates somebody, everything would be eliminated by process of elimination! Wow, that was deep!

The line in the song that I have the most problem with is not the legs part, it is the last line. That little sentence that was obviously put in there because they couldn't think of another movement line that rhymed. The last line says, "That's what it's all about." That phrase has to be one of the most overused phrases of the century. Everywhere you turn you hear, "That's what it's all about." John Madden will be commentating on a football play, "You take the ball and run it across the goal line... Now that's what it's all about." Then he goes on to say, "When the lineman stands there and takes it on the chin... That's what it's all about." Then in the very next sentence he will say, "When the quarterback drops back and fakes a hand-off, and then tosses it to a half-back and he runs it twenty yards... That's what it's all about." Listen to me people - it can't be all about everything!

I'm watching a tractor pull on television. Don't laugh, we don't have a lot of programming choices in Alabama! There was that line again. The announcer is interviewing the winner of the pull. The winner, an obviously educated man (I say that tongue in cheek) blurts, "Well we just tried to drive the tractor over the finish line faster than everybody else...

That's what it's all about." The announcer closes the program almost as if he was not listening to his winner and says, "There you have it folks... Another great guy who knows how to drive a tractor...and that's what it's all about." I flip to the twenty-four hour fishing channel. There it is again. "Catching a good fish... Now that's what it's all about."

To be real honest, it must be what people say when they can't think of anything else to positive to say. It has to be the new "uh-huh" for the journalistic world, because certainly educated, thinking people must know that everything can't be what it's all about. The nature of the statement suggests a singular thing being most important. The nature of the word that and it seems to mean a singular item. I could be wrong, I have yet to finish Senior English, but I certainly don't think that you can't have multiple "most important" things. That really goes without saying! But I said it anyway, so there.

Here I am complaining about a statement and you are saying, "Hey my footless friend, what is it all about then?" I'm glad you asked. Because questions like that are really what it's all about! I'm sorry, I had to say that just for fun! I have a lot of time to think about these things. While you're busy putting on socks and shoes, I'm thinking about things. Lot's of things. Like the hidden meanings of Egyptian hieroglyphics and what the secret ingredients in SPAM are. But let me get back to my point. What is it all about? Let's first define the word it. Say the word is referring to all of life here on earth. Our time spent breathing, eating, sleeping, school, jobs, religion, families, and friends. What is it all about? What is the purpose of it all? It's about... (drum roll please)... connecting. Connecting is using the tools we are given to connect to each other's soul. Connecting is reaching beyond the walls, languages, oceans, crutches, and metal wheelchair's that separate us, and touching each others' soul. Connecting is the realization that we are not all that different. It is realizing that we all have fears and we all have insecurities. It is the knowledge that we all have a need to be seen, loved, held, and valued. Yes, valued! It does not matter whether you are an infant or a senior citizen, you want and need to be connected. Yes, you need to be connected with. You need to know that as you travel through this thing called life, from the point of birth, to the point of death, you have connected and been connected with.

I mentioned the R word (religion) in the last paragraph. I know that word is a bit controversial in the business that I am in. I am allowed to talk about anything I want to... but I must leave out religion. I'm waiting for the day you will have to replace that word with "beeeeeeeeep." We will be able to shout profanities or write them in bold print, but we will have to disguise the R word. People say that religion is too divisive! But is it? In its purest form, when you consider it, religion is all about connecting. It has always been about man attempting to connect with the supernatural. And I'm all for that. I believe in that connection, too. I certainly need that connection and I certainly need to feel, know, and understand somehow that there is more beyond this world, and that I have somehow connected with the more. It may not be right now, but I'll bet before you leave this world you will have a desire to connect further too.

So that's my take on it. And I am an expert! Why? Because it's my book. Didn't they tell you the rule? No? Okay here it is: If you are from out of town, have a briefcase, and have written a book, you are an expert! That's the rule. I'm sorry you weren't told earlier, but now you know. So, as an expert, I will conclude this chapter by saying, "Connecting with each other, mortal and immortal...that's really what life is all about."

This is a new day that God has given me, I can use it for
good or I can waste it, but I must always remember...
whatever I do with today...that I
have exchanged a day of my life for it.

-*Anonymous*

To ADD Or Not To ADD That is The Question

Certainly adversity builds character...but it also reveals it. - Robert K. Lash

My mom said that I had ADD Attention Deficit Disorder. I'm glad I didn't have ADHD (Attention Deficit - Hyperactivity Disorder). It would have been a bear to have a need to run around incessantly and not have the ability to do it! So I guess I was fortunate. My Dad often said I had AC/DC, but dad is an old rocker, so he talks that way a lot. And really Angus is much taller than me! But I do own a pair of black shorts and suspenders. I meet a lot of students with this ADD and ADHD stuff. These disorders are real, and I do not want to make light of them in any way, but... I wonder sometimes if I people really have it, or if they just don't want to pay attention. Hey, it's a valid question.

It is said that those with ADD can't focus on one thing. I prefer to believe it is more like a computer with a lot of RAM. Those with ADD are simply more mentally multi-tasking. They are focusing on everything at the same time, and will probably process everything as they get time to pull it back out of the hard drive...and they will eventually process it. There are times when I have thought that a group of students were not listening to anything I said, but later find out that they could repeat back everything I said. Interesting.

People with these problems often talk out loud. There is a reason. Talking out loud allows us to focus on what we are saying, because we are hearing and saying it. The sound of my own voice helps drown out the things that are vying for my attention. Thinking alone doesn't use enough brain capacity and I could be quickly distracted if I only thought about stuff. I am an out-loud thinker. Without it I would be distracted by the other stuff that is floating around in my head. You know, like why do carnival workers smell like embalming fluid? Or why did Mr. Webster cruelly put an s in the word lisp? And how do fish sleep with their eyes open and why can't I?

The key to speaking to someone with ADD or ADHD is to be so visual, so big, so larger-than-life, and so vocal, that you are utilizing all their mental working RAM by their simple act of looking at you. Teachers of these guys and gals have it the toughest! They need to be illustrative, entertaining, funny, and off-the-wall, and at the same time they are being informative and educational. I'm glad I'm not a teacher. I wouldn't want to work for the minuscule pay package they receive and be in the respect- less environment they are in.

Maybe you are a person who struggles to stay focused on one thing. I'm sorry. I understand. If you knew how hard it was for me, you would know that I really understand. But there comes a time when we have to take control of our own minds. There comes a time when you and I will have to realize that our future is in our hands. If we want to be successful in life we will have to get control of our minds. They tell me that you never really grow out of this, so I better learn to work with it. And you better also. Start by realizing that your very busy mind can be a great asset or a great liability. You can let yourself go and become a random mental computer locked up in a continuous loop, or you can choose to use that highly creative mind to bring success to your life.

A good friend of mine (a self proclaimed poster child for ADD) often says, "It is so weird to know that I now get paid for what I used to get school detentions for. The same mind that often got me expelled from school now equips me to go back into those schools and entertain the students! Life is too crazy." So, obviously, you can turn this so called "disorder" around. There are things you can do to help yourself. You can fill your mind with positive things. You may have to fill your room with motivational posters, or rid yourself of influences that will distract you - especially the bad influences. You know what they are, I don't have to list the negative things in your sphere of influence. For every age group there are a different set of distractions, you must choose to remove yourself from the negative attractions and negative distractions.

Become a strong person. Choose to take control of your life. Take control over what situations you can. There are certainly a lot of you who have been placed in horrible situations at home, with family, or at work, and you have no control over those things. There will come a time when those negative influences will be gone from your life. All things pass. What matters is that we not allow ourselves to be permanently messed up by them. We must focus on the future and not allow ourselves to be sucked in to the mess.

I choose to use this day for good. It may not be easy. I chose to use this day for the positive although it may be difficult in this negative society. I will not waste this day. I will make the most of this day. I will learn and grow today, because tomorrow will soon be here and I want to be equipped to experience success. I would rather live in victory than live in misery and blame. I will not give up or give in!

The highest courage is to dare to be your own self in the face of adversity. Choosing right over wrong, ethics over convenience, and truth over popularity... these are the choices that measure your life. Travel the path of integrity without looking back, for there is never a wrong time to do a right thing.

-Anonymous

Dumped On My First Date

You christen a new ship by smashing a bottle over the nose before the first ride. You should not try this with a new pony - I thought the children would never quit crying. -Tim Jones

Another campout, another year, and this time a beautiful young lady was camping a few sites down from us. Jamie had a great little smile, beautiful brown hair and brown eyes, and best of all she took a liking to me. What can I say, I have a way with women! We talked and played, and of course fished. I shared all my secrets as a virtual professional fisherman and she listened intently. One night her family was going to the carnival and invited me to go. I think it was at the local fire house or maybe it was at Catholic church. Maybe it was Our Lady of Firehouse Saints! I can't really remember.

It had been raining real hard that day so I took a

wheelchair along with me. I do great on my hands in dry weather, but I tend to get a little water logged when I teeter through puddles! So she pushed me around and we had the time of our lives. We went from ride to ride and game to game. I tried to win her a big stuffed animal but was not very successful. I did manage to beat the guy at "Guess your age, or weight". But somehow that stuffed orange and black carrot was not what I had in mind as a gift for my carnival queen.

The rain had finally stopped and we were going to take one last ride on the Tilt-O-Whirl before heading back to the campground. She was pushing me quite fast across that grass covered church yard as we came upon a big puddle. I tried to warn her, but she said, "Yeah-yeah," as we headed into the shallow puddle. I'm not sure if it was one of those carnival electrical lines or just the mud catching on the front wheels, but the next thing you know the wheelchair stopped hard... and I continued. As usual, head first I plowed into the mud. She laughed and laughed. I personally did not find it as amusing. But as I look back now it was hilarious!

Some helpful bystanders took me to the side of the Bingo Hall and hosed me off. I returned to the campground, soaked to the gills. That's how I got "dumped" on my first date. I saw her very few times after that week, but it was fun while it lasted and I'm sure she has told the story many times to her friends, as I have mine.

Laughter often comes at the expense of someone. Nobody would think the Three Stooges were funny if they just walked down a sidewalk. But if you put a ladder in the hands of Moe, a saw in the hands of Larry, and a hammer in the hands of Curly, you know you're in for a treat. Somebody would get it in the head with a ladder! Somebody would be faced with a saw! Somebody would get knocked in the head with a hammer! It would be funny! And we would laugh! Well it would be funny as long as we were not the ones getting it in the head. But can you imagine the stress that could be alleviated from our lives if we could learn to laugh while we were getting it in the back of the head with a ladder?

Think about it. When we become the master of our own emotions, we win. When we become, as the Rotarians say, "...Too large to be shaken by the things around us," we are truly the victors in life. And what a victory it is. I think it was the Rotarians... It could have been the Optimists or the Kiwanis Club. I almost joined the Optimists, but I wasn't sure they were going to stay around. Now I'm certainly not saying that I am happy with every health condition and or situation that I find myself in, but I am saying that when I find a way to release laughter into the situation, it makes everyone involved feel better. It makes me feel better, and that's a good thing.

I used to pray that I would have no dreams because I often
had bad ones. I quit praying for the dreams to
stop and started praying for good dreams to come...
ones that could one day come true.

-*Chapman Clay Williams*

Live out of your dreams - not out of your fears.

-*Anonymous*

I Wish I Was An...

When Danny was in the Hospital I would pull him around in a wagon and he would entertain the other children and nurses by singing I Wish I was an Oscar Mayer Weiner...and many other songs. He's always had a flair for entertaining and he's certainly not shy! -Sandi Frasier

I have a unique singing voice. Some people would call it weird! I was born in New York, but I spent my high school years in Alabama, which means my accent sounds like a cross between Danny DeVito and Jeff Foxworthy. In fact I look like a cross between those two! And as a resident of the south, let me simply add that everything Jeff has said about Rednecks is true. I am now semi-proud to be one of them. I don't know how it happened. It just did. Living in Alabama kind of wears on you. You begin to adapt to your surroundings. It's like a scab. It hurts, but you enjoy picking at it when you're bored.

I can speak fluent Yankee and fluent Redneck. I guess that makes me bi-lingual!

Some of you know that I recorded my first musical CD when I was a sophomore in High School. It's not the greatest CD in the world but my mom really likes it, and I do sell quite a few. Have you bought one yet? Please do, remember I'm saving for the new car! My love for performing music actually developed in New York when I was nine. A country singer took a special interest in me. My dad had taken an early retirement from Kodak and was working part time for retirement home in Hilton, New York. Part of his responsibilities were to set up, for the neighborhood, community programs that were sponsored by the retirement home. One of the visiting musical artists was Josie Waverly. Josie is a wonderful lady full of hope and joy. Her performance gets everyone involved, including the kids. It was during this time of interaction that we had the occasion to meet. Josie called all the kids up to the stage. The plan was to teach them to line dance. She lined all the kids up, one by one, and then she came to me. How do you teach a kid with no legs to line dance? But without missing a beat she said, "And you come up here with me!" As the kids kicked their legs, I swung my arms, as they scooted their boots, I scooted my bottom. After the concert I asked for her autograph. I even got to sing a song for her. Before you knew it, a friendship had sprung that has lasted to this day. It wasn't long before Josie put me on her local show schedule and I got my first chances at playing and singing in front of crowds.

It is true that when you plant encouragement you receive encouragement. It was Christmas time and I found myself at a mall looking for that perfect gift for my family. I was also there because Josie was doing a Christmas show on the center mall stage. She called me out of the crowd that night and I took the microphone to sing I Believe There Are Angels Among Us. It's one of those tear jerkers that really moves you, especially at Christmas time. The crowd applauded and Josie finished the show. She telephoned my mother at home later that evening. She explained that the road life had gotten very hard and she was ready to walk away from her dream, and that night was to have been the end of it. She cried as she explained how that night my song had spoken to her. She knew that she could go on. Since that time she opened Josie's Country Jukebox and has helped many children through benefits and charities. At that time in my life I had little idea of how I might be used to motivate people. For Josie and I the motivation has been reciprocal. I cannot begin to say how Josie has impacted my life.

Although you will probably never see me line dance on American Idol, I have enjoyed sharing the stage with world famous country groups like Alabama. I've even been invited back stage at the Grand Ole Opry. Few New Yorkers can say that. It's amazing what a little encouragement can do. I'm certainly thankful for those who have encouraged me through the years, and encouragement can help you too. So if you haven't read into what I am saying right now, here it is: Dare to follow your dream and stick with it even though the path is hard. Live out your dreams - not your fears.

My singing developed quite a bit after we moved to this beloved southern state, thus it is slightly country-fied. I sound like Hank Williams when I sing, but my brother says I sound more like a cat in a blender! I have never heard a cat in a blender so I really have no reference point in which to comment from. I often strap on my guitar at events and start into a song and people do a double take. I can see their eyes saying, "Is that his real voice?" Yep! Sure is! No milli-vanilli here, it's all me! The worlds shortest Yankee-country singer! I'm a little mixed up that way. We all are. Who isn't a combination of their mom, dad, friends, family, area they live in, and favorite cartoon super-hero. I believe the reason that so many people watch those stupid daytime talk shows is, because no matter how messed up they feel their life is, they can turn on Springer and find people who area lot more messed up than them! We are all a little Heinz 57 at times. We all have those areas in our lives we really don't want exposed, but somehow they seem to be the areas that come blasting to the forefront, only to be laughed at by people with their own set of absurdities.

The truth is that we laugh at people and point out their absurdities because we are trying to distract people from noticing our own absurdities. Well at least that is my opinion. And you must remember that I am an expert, right? Hey I've got the briefcase next to me, and I am typing this from a hotel room in, ah, well somewhere, I forget right now. It would do us all good to treat people the way we want to be treated. It would be great if we could all love each other as fellow citizens of a messed up world. We can. At least I would like to think that we can. Maybe some of us need to be brought to our knees before we will change our superior attitudes. Hey, I'm game with that. Let it be! I'm saying that like I have some ability to make it happen. Hey, I can wish.

That song, Don't Laugh at Me, is a favorite of mine. I learned it first hand from Peter Yarrow of the infamous Peter, Paul, and Mary one time. And no, Peter, Paul, and Mary are not the creators of the Almond Joy bar! They were the PBS Folk Music Special people! In February of 2000, Peter was giving a free concert at the University of Alabama, but you had to call in for tickets. Well before I even heard about the concert the tickets had been given away. My chance to hear a childhood idle had been crushed. My mom can be a little persuasive at times. Have you met her? She shared a little of my story with the promoter, who asked for me to write a letter and fax it to their office. The Dean of the school gave the letter to Peter. He read it and said, "I want that boy on my stage." Wow! Here is my big break. This could lead to an audition for the group! Hey, Paul Stokey can't sing and play guitar forever! I could be the newest member of PP&M! We packed my guitar and headed of to UAB!

I will never forget the introduction in the backstage dressing room. Peter got down on his knees, and with his warm and friendly swagger gave me a big hug. It felt like he was an old friend. He explained to me that he was there to launch a program in elementary schools across the country. It was going to help children understand and respect each others differences. It was that night that he taught me the song Don't Laugh at Me. Learning that song from Peter was truly one of the highlights of my life.

I sing that song almost everywhere I go. The words just sum up what I want to say so often. Some nights I close my show by picking up my guitar and strumming the intro to it. I've watched students, even the tough guys with tears in their eyes join me as I sing, "I'm the little boy with glasses, the one they call a geek, I'm a little girl who never smiles, because I have braces on my teeth, I'm the kid on every playground, who is always chosen last." Can you relate to any of those? I have seen adults reach for their handkerchief as verse two proclaims, "I'm a single mother, who is trying to overcome her past, I'm fat, I'm thin, I'm short, I'm tall, I'm deaf, I'm blind, Hey aren't we all?" I've experience the union of souls as the chorus rings out, "Don't laugh at me, don't call me names, don't get your pleasure from my pain, In God's eyes were all the same, someday we'll all have perfect wings, Don't laugh at me." I anxiously wait on the someday. How about you?

We are all broken from time to time. We must lift each other up during our good times and pray that someone will be there for us in our low times. I don't really think I need to add anything more to that, do you? You get the point, right? I thought so.

Some people choose to dream about success... while others
wake up and work hard for it.
It is time to get out of bed and get to work!
-*Danny Frasier*

You Can Have A Lot Of Fun With No Legs

Sometimes for fun, I go into a shoe store and just wait for some one to ask if they can help me find something. I just smile as if I am dreaming. -Danny Frasier

I love to walk up to counters when the person behind that counter did not see me. I just start talking to the person. I wish I could see their face. I know they must be thinking they are experiencing some sort of weird X-Files phenomenon. They can hear a voice but there seems to be nobody there. Hotels have special rooms for people like me. They have two of those little security door viewers. You know the ones you are supposed to look out of before you open the door. This supposedly lets you identify the person before you let them in. Have you ever looked out of the lower one? For security

81

indow is useless, unless the hotel staff mem-
₃ a name tags on their belt buckle. "Hey mom,
ᴜy named Levi's 501!"

admit that I have had fun with my situation for
years. What else can you do? You can't just sit there. When I
was about a year old they gave me a square board with wheels
on it to encourage me to crawl. They had to watch me like a
hawk to prevent me from scooting out the door and down the
driveway. A few times I made it! My first actual prosthesis was
a bucket-like seat called a Para-podium. It held me upright on
a round base. It allowed me to spin in place by swinging my
arms, if I got off balance it could twirl me into another room.
Who knew that I would be the prototype for weebles! Yeah, I
wobbled but I didn't fall down.

My parents were was rather inventive. They designed a
walker that was made out of my Pipeworks set. It wasn't
much more than a few pieces of polished PVC pipe, but it
worked for me. They say that necessity is the mother of inven-
tion. They never found out who the father was... makes you
wonder... doesn't it? I think it was ingenuity! I am thankful for
innovativeness and encouragement from the people around
me. They have helped me find ways of overcoming the seem-
ingly impossible. Encouragement always breeds more produc-
tivity than discouragement! Have you found that to be true?
Last week I was in Florida to do a program for a group of stu-

dents. Before the event they took me out to a restaurant for dinner. As we left the restaurant a huge white tour bus filled with senior citizens pulled up to the curb. Yes! Party time! Here is my chance to have a little fun in the senior citizen state. I scurried to the front wheel of the bus and slid my lower torso right up to that big bus tire. I sat up on my elbows and waited for the AARP Club to disembark. Two ladies came walking out the door that is directly in front of that wheel and their eyes about popped out of their heads. I would say that their hair turned purple... but it already was. I looked up and said, "Excuse me ladies, can you ask the driver to pull this rig up a few more feet? I seem to be stuck?" The laughter from the group around me signaled to these ladies that it was a joke. I would hate to be responsible for shortening the life of a ninety-five year old. They both laughed, so in a way, my little joke lengthened their life. Laughter does that!

Laughter is great medicine. But unfortunately it can't be bottled and sold. I am waiting for the day that a doctor gives a patient a prescription and he has to take it down to the local record store. It could read, "Two hours of comedy before each meal and a television bloopers video every night before bed time." I can imagine going to my medicine cabinet and seeing Tylenol, Aspirin, cough syrup, and a stack of Mark Lowry, Ken Davis, Mike Williams, Robert G. Lee, and Chonda Pierce videos. Now that's my kind of medicine!

Maybe you need to laugh a little more. It would do you a world of good. Yeah, just to sit back and belly laugh until your sides hurt. It could add years to your life. It will certainly add life to your years. So go ahead and buy a good funny video or comedy recording. If nobody is home, make a prank call to a friend. It is better to do it to a friend, because caller ID can get you busted with a stranger! But whatever you choose to do... laugh hard today. Life is too short not to laugh! And sometimes it is too long not too laugh.

Watch your thoughts; they become your words.
Watch your words they become your actions.
Watch your actions; they become your habits.
Watch your habits; they become your character.
Watch your character for it becomes your destiny.

-Dietrich Bonhoeffer

Where Do We Go From Here

I want to get a full body tattoo of me...only thinner!
-Steven Wright

Well as you can tell the hope of being a professional fisherman has kind of fallen apart. My application for a starting position with the Chicago Bulls was not returned. I didn't get the job as a counter worker at McDonalds either. They said something about a minimum height requirement and OSHA regulations. Whatever! So I am embarking on a new dream... I want to be a professional roller coaster rider, but until that comes through I will continue doing what I do now...helping people learn to laugh. Helping people learn to look on the bright side and helping people realize that they have a lot to be thankful for. This is the kind of work that brings purpose to my life. And we all need purpose!

I often get the opportunity to go into public schools and share my stories with the students. I love to do that, and they seem to like it okay too. But it is an easy crowd. They have to love you. Seriously... you just got them out of class for an hour... you are a hero. I enjoy helping students realize their potential. I guess I just like connecting. That simple act of making some kind of emotional contact with others in a way that is above and beyond the inadvertent nod in the hall. I love it when I can go away from a place and know that I was there for a purpose. There is a joy in knowing that what you do, and who you are, is blessing other people. And everyone has that ability. Whether it is one person at a time, or speaking to a group of five thousand, we all have the ability to share our life stories and connect and encourage.

So like I say, until that roller coaster position opens up I will be an encourager. Danny Frasier, Professional Encourager! I believe that has a nice ring to it. Who are you? No, not what do you do? Who are you? On the inside? Are you a giver or a taker? Are you an encourager or discourager? Do you motivate or do you constipate? Maybe I shouldn't have said it that way. Are you stuffing or potatoes? Does your entrance into a room bring about anticipation or despair? Can you laugh at the follies of your own making? I hope so. I hope you choose to bring joy! I hope you choose to lift peo- ple up! I hope you learn to laugh at yourself instead of others! I hope you are a stork of goodness! When that happens the world will be changed because of you. Well, I should say, "The world will be changed by you, too." Yeah, along with the coaster thing, I plan on changing the world a little myself!

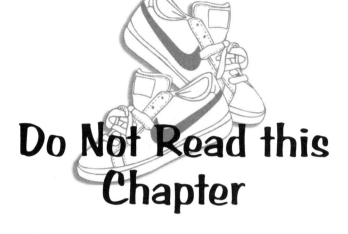

Do Not Read this Chapter

WARNING: Do not read this chapter without the permission of a parent or guardian. What I am about to say is illegal for me to say in some places, namely the public school system. I want to inform you of that right now. I certainly don't want to violate your right to be uniformed about my entire life story. There are a few people who would not allow me to say what I am going to say because they feel it might infringe upon your right to make your own choice. They feel that somehow my words might impede your ability to think for yourself. So, as a warning, let me say that you may want to just close the book and walk away. I have to say this because I know that a lot of people who read this book are students. But if you are over eighteen and capable of making your own decision as to how you would feel about the rest of my story please read on. If you are under eighteen you should get the permission of a parent or guardian before reading the following paragraphs.

I believe in connecting. I said that earlier. So I make no apology for what I am about to say. I understand that there are people who cannot see things the way I do, and for those people I feel very sorry. I mean that. I feel that my ability to look positively upon life stems from my ability to feel a certainty about the future. A future where all the wrongs in this world will be righted. That includes my having a new set of legs. It includes my being able to legitimately ask the whereabouts of my shoes. To be honest, if there is not more to this life than what we have today, then this life is pretty shallow.

To me it seems almost a cruel joke, to be given self awareness only to have it stripped from me upon death. Gaining fine things, family, relationships, and memories seem nothing more than a horrible prank if there is nothing beyond the grave, if it is all over when the heart stops beating. So that is why I am concerned with connecting to something more. I believe that God-connecting is my only hope in bringing real and ultimate purpose to my existence.

People place their faith in many things, and I certainly am not going to knock their ideas. Rather I prefer to tell you where I find connection to God. I told you earlier that my parents were church type people, but that really has little to do with my personal beliefs. Their faith has certainly influenced me, but definitely did not force my choice in any area. My faith is mine and your faith is yours. And though we are influenced by that which is around us, it is our choice as to what we believe in.

My personal beliefs began to come into play when I was quite young, through the little life lessons that the children's television shows would teach about how we need to make good decisions. I came to understand that I certainly made a lot of bad decisions. And I really enjoyed making them. I was good at it. But self concerned existence only lead to a more self infatuated living style. It certainly never brings about connecting. Selfishness always brings about brokenness. At a young age I understood that I needed help to get my heart in order.

My personal faith story blossomed when my neighbor asked me if I had ever been saved. Saved is one of those words that church people often use. It basically means rescued! It has to do with coming to a point in your life where you realize there is a God and that you want to connect to Him. When Don and his wife Patty asked me that question I said that I had not. I don't remember too much about the exact moment. I do remember their kneeling down on the floor beside me. I asked God to come into my life and connect with me. I asked for God to forgive me for inappropriate behaviors of my heart and life. I asked for Jesus Christ to come in to my heart and connect with my life. There was no band that played. There were no angels singing around the room. I asked God to save me, and according to how I interpret the Bible... God did. I am very thankful for the neighbor who helped me find this God-connection! Ironically, Don has become a good friend of mine through the years and wrote most of the songs on my first CD.

Sure, I know that there are other theological options and alternatives, but they never really answered all the questions. Some taught me how to live with myself. Some taught me how to live with others. Some taught me that I was to consider all the things in this life to be unreal, as if only a dream. Others offered me an opportunity to earn a spot in the eternal, like I could really do that. But it was only the teachings of Jesus Christ that fully answered the questions of real connection with God. It was only Jesus Christ that offered an example of what it meant to be resurrected, to live beyond this world. So I'm going with the only one who has given any evidence that His way of connecting to God brought resurrection. Call me brainless if you want, but it seems to me to be a no brainer! Call me narrow minded if you want. That's okay. I feel rather informed and connected.

So what about you? Have you reached a place in your

life where you want to know there is a reason for your life? Have you ever felt like there must be something more? Have you come to a place where you feel this life is a rip-off if you have to close your eyes on it all in the end? What handicap do you desire to put aside some day? Do you ever secretly wish that you could connect with the eternal? You are not alone. I meet people every day who feel the same way. Now I admit that I am not the most "world traveled" or "universally informed," but I do know that finding a connection to God through Jesus Christ has changed my life. It has given me a purpose filled life. I don't believe that you can really live until you have dealt with the death question. You can't really live until you have your eternal future worked out. You may want to do as I did many years ago, humble yourself before the Creator in prayer and ask Him to make your heart new. Ask Him to invade your life and mind. Ask Him to give you a purpose in living. Ask Him for the forgiveness that comes through connecting with the cross of Christ. You may also want to find a good church to help you in your spiritual life. I highly recommend it.

To make a mistake is human; to stay humble is common-
place; to be able to laugh at yourself is maturity.
-William A. Ward

In Closing

Don't run with scissors unless they have rounded edges. Never play with fire unless that is your job. Don't litter. Recycle! Never put your tongue on a frozen flag pole. Keep your shirt on. Never drink the milk after the expiration date. Don't believe everything you see on television. In fact, don't believe much of anything you see on television. Be thankful for everything. Make lots of friends. Take time to fish in a pond. Build a snowman every chance you get. Write a letter to the President. Play at the beach and build a sandcastle at low tide just to see the waves take it away. Eat at a Waffle House once or twice, it's a cultural experience you don't want to miss. Make a yearly trip to the cemetery just to think about the future. And in the words of a great country music song..."I hope you dance!" But do not settle for dancing the Hokey Pokey, that isn't what it's all about.

The End

For now!

Resource List

I recommend the following websites as great places to find
the medicine of laughter...

www.christiancomedian.com

www.marklowry.com

www.chonda.org

www.kendavis.com

www.robertglee.com

www.paulaldrich.com

www.sheeplaughs.com

www.gordondouglas.com

I also recommend the great work of...

Joni and Friends www.joniandfriends.org

New Missions www.lifeofachild.com

Please visit my own website at www.dannyfrasier.com